Three Wise Fools

A fantasy on the Nativity

Margaret Franks

Radius (The Religious Drama Society of Great Britain) works with churches, community groups and the theatre to promote drama that explores faith. The membership is drawn from all denominations and reflects a broad Christian understanding.

Radius achieves its objectives through the active encouragement and publishing of new plays, training workshops in aspects of dramatised presentation and a summer school. It has an extensive library of plays and books on theatre.

For more information write to:
Radius
58-60 Lincoln Road
Peterborough PE1 2RZ
England

Telephone: +44 (0) 1733 565 613
E-mail: info@radius.org.uk
Website: www.radius.org.uk

The play **Three Wise Fools** was written when an amateur group, called Teamact, asked for a Christmas play. Not wanting to repeat the usual and somewhat hackneyed versions of the Nativity, I felt we could explore some of the more intriguing aspects of the story.

I have always been fascinated by the wise men of the gospel who developed into the three kings of popular myth. Why did they come to Bethlehem? What exactly were they expecting, or at least hoping for? I was very attracted to T S Eliot's poem *The Journey of the Magi*, as many of my generation were, and that provided me with some clues as to their journey and their possible doubts.

In an uncomfortable waiting situation they could well have had some crisis of faith. They did not, of course, meet the shepherds in the Biblical account, but meeting them in this situation could have further challenged their assumptions and expectations.

Margaret Franks

About the author

Margaret Franks is a former teacher enjoying retirement in rural Suffolk. She has written plays, usually for people she knows, since the age of fourteen. In the late eighties and early nineties she was a member of a group of amateurs drawn from several churches in an Anglican team in the Mildenhall district. She wrote and directed several religious plays for them, which toured the local churches.

Some of the plays have been published: the first was *Amos and his all-singing, all-dancing, athletic artistes,* another was the Bible dramatisation *A donkey's tale* inspired by the story of Balaam and his talking donkey. Since then she has had a further publication with the same publishers, Moorleys Print and Publishing in Ilkeston, Derbyshire. This is a book of four short plays called *Meet the Saints,* each one an affectionate, if not entirely serious, look at the patron saints of the UK.

Characters

Melchior
He is elderly, philosophical, a little melancholy, but with a dry sense of humour that comes with age and experience.

Balthasar
Is lean, intellectual and a worrier.

Caspar
Is younger, sturdy, bustling and managing.

The Recording Angel
Can be male or female.

First, Second and Third Shepherds
Can be male or female.

Other Shepherds
At least two, but could be any number, male or female.

The play which is set in a waiting room is a fantasy, and the humour should be allowed to surface. In the original production the characters were dressed traditionally, but they could just as well be in modern dress.

Running time: approximately 35 minutes

Three Wise Fools

A boring, dreary waiting room. A line of 6-8 hard, identical chairs are placed from left to right at the back of the stage. By the far right chair there is a small, low table covered with magazines and newspapers. On the back wall are posters in varying degrees of wear and tear.

On the farthest chair right sits Melchior, patiently leafing through the magazines. He is elderly, philosophical, a little melancholy, but with a dry sense of humour that comes with age and experience. On the two chairs furthest left sit Balthasar and Caspar with their arms folded, tense and fidgety. Caspar is younger, sturdy, bustling and managing. Balthasar is lean, intellectual and a worrier.

In the original production the three kings/wise men were dressed traditionally as gorgeously as any Christmas card, long robes, ornaments, headdresses etc. However, they could just as well be in modern western dress or dressed as modern Arabs, according to the creative ideas of the director. They should look striking and have the presence of those used to command. However, they are not commanding anything now.

The situation is not under their control. The action begins with a longish silence while Balthasar and Caspar fidget, yawn, gaze impatiently around the room, drum their fingers etc.

Balthasar Are you sure this is the place?

Caspar *(A gusty sigh of exasperation)* Fourteen!

Balthasar I beg your pardon?

Caspar Fourteen! That is the fourteenth time you have asked me! And this is the fourteenth and last time I shall say YES! Yes! Yes! Yes! Yes! Of course this is the place! The omens, the signs, our calculations, the palace astrologers, the time - yes! Especially the time. This is the place. We all agreed.

Balthasar Perhaps we made a mistake?

Caspar Mistake? I made no mistake.

Balthasar It wouldn't be the first time.

Caspar What do you mean?

Balthasar We went wrong before.

Caspar We went wrong? *(Remembering hastily)* No we didn't! That was - that was a detour. Just a detour. Besides we couldn't go past without calling to pay our respects. It wouldn't have been polite. They are family after all.

Balthasar Family! It's always family! Is there any royal family between here and Babylon you are not related to?

Caspar No. No, I don't think so.

Balthasar That's one of the reasons it has taken us so long. I never dreamed it would take us so long. Paying our respects to your family has added months, years to our trek. *(Sadly)* I have been away so long. I don't feel I am simply on a journey. I feel I have gone into exile.

Caspar   What about me? How do you think I feel? Wondering what sort of mess and muddle they'll all be getting into without me. None of them, none of them can read the simplest of instructions, and heaven knows I left enough of them, without getting it wrong and getting into a muddle! *(Sighs)* It'll all be waiting for me when I get back. One big muddle. *(Pause)* Still, I'm not complaining about the journey. After all, it's cheaper staying with relatives.

Balthasar   I'm not complaining about the journey – except, except that it took so long.

Melchior   *(Looking up from his magazine)* Longer than could have been expected. Not a good time to start out. *(Goes back to his reading)*

Balthasar   Well! That was hardly our fault.

Melchior   *(Shaking his head murmuring as he turns a page)* . . . In the bleak midwinter.

Caspar   He didn't have to come.

Balthasar   *(Gloomily)* None of us did.

Caspar   *(After a pause)* Yes . . . yes, we did. We had to come.

Balthasar   You know I've never enjoyed administration. I always yearned after the contemplative life. All I ever wanted was to be left alone with my scrolls, the ancient wisdom and the stars. But that was my undoing. If I had busied myself more with the affairs of state I should never have stumbled across the sign. It was, it was like hearing a trumpet call! A summons! A call to arms! I was gripped with an urgency I had never experienced.

Caspar   I know, I know! I felt an enthusiasm I had only ever felt before for my full granaries and balanced accounts! But it was more than that. There was something else, a feeling that the old satisfactions were not enough, the old ways were beginning to fall apart.

Melchior (*Puts down paper and stares ahead*) The old dispensation was no longer enough.

Caspar Something stirring - something I was told I shouldn't miss.

Balthasar Like seeing the light of the sun over the horizon - before the dawn.

Caspar That's it! That's it! The light! We were drawn irresistibly towards this vision of the light!

Balthasar (*Sighing*) But visions fade in the bitter cold, the rude wind's loud lament! Those filthy lodgings and their exorbitant prices!

Caspar (*Losing his excitement and remembering*) And the camel drivers were always thieving and abusive. Not much contemplation there!

Melchior (*Still looking ahead remembering*) It was better travelling at night.

Balthasar At least then we could still see the stars.

Caspar Sleeping in snatches; waking in the dark; fumbling about.

Melchior Like lame men who stumble. (*Sighs and goes back to reading his magazine*)

Balthasar (*Nodding sadly*) Visions fade. (*A sad pause, but then Caspar brightens up*)

Caspar But we didn't stop! We didn't stop! Not once did we even mention going back. No, we kept on going! And we've arrived. We have achieved our journey's end. That's something!

Balthasar (*Gloomily*) But it may all be for nothing. It's so hard to feel sure you have made the right interpretation. Signs, yes! But meaning - that's another thing. We're only human. We need some reassurance, something more concrete than a sign or a prophecy. Certainty, that's what we crave.

Caspar   *(Exasperated)* If only something would happen now. It's the waiting that's so hard. After all our efforts and striving, it's the waiting that is so difficult to endure. If something happens soon, we shall know – one way or another.

The Recording Angel comes in from the left

Caspar   *(Rising)* At last!

Angel   *(Absorbed in papers on a clipboard. Stops, looks up and sees them)* Ah, gentlemen. *(Smiles brightly)* Not long now.

Caspar   Not long, not long! This is a mismanaged business.

Balthasar   But . . . but something is happening now?

Angel   Oh, yes! Most definitely. A happening of the first importance.

Balthasar   That would be good to know - if it were true.

Angel   True? True, gentlemen? Have you really come all this way doubting?

Balthasar   *(Hurriedly)* No! By no means. It's only that the vision fades, you know.   The initial brightness and confidence; and it's hard to keep your first certainty when the way is so long and, and . . .

Melchior   . . . and in the bleak midwinter.

Caspar   And then to actually arrive and not to be able to take another promising step, and still not know! Why are we waiting?

Angel   The fullness of time, gentlemen. *(Slightly shocked)* I rather expected you to know that.

Caspar   Ah, yes, the time. *(Walks up and down)* We had the time worked out. Reams of astrological calculations! That's how I was sure we had come to the right place. I never do anything without planning. That's what I can't understand. The journey was planned down to the last crust of bread and spare saddle thong. And it all went exactly as planned.

Balthasar Apart from the detour.

Caspar Apart from the detour. But the timing was right. We arrived in time. That's what I can't understand.

Angel *(Gently)* I have to remind you of one thing, gentlemen.

Caspar And that is?

Angel These are not your plans.

Caspar *(Nonplussed and sitting down in the middle of the row)* Oh!

Melchior starts reading again

Angel *(Brightly)* Faith and patience, gentlemen. All will be revealed. Now if you'll excuse me there are some people I have to contact. *(Begins to leave across stage to right)*

Caspar People? People? You mean there are others apart from ourselves?

Angel *(Stopping, surprised)* Of course! Other signs, other journeys, *(pointedly)* other people waiting.

Caspar Well, I just hope you have room for them all. It's going to be a little crowded in here.

Angel Oh, they won't have to wait long. They'll probably go straight in.

Caspar *(Jumping to his feet)* What?

Balthasar That's hardly fair!

Caspar   We were here first.

Angel   Ah yes. But the first shall be last and the last first.

Caspar   On whose orders?

Angel   The new dispensation. From what I heard, gentlemen, that is why you came. You were tired and dissatisfied with the old one.

Balthasar   It does seem rather unreasonable.

Caspar   *(Furious)* Unreasonable? What happened to order? What happened to rank and hierarchy? What happened to respect for authority and power? What happened to ceremony? Hmmm?

Melchior   *(Suddenly)* Not many wise men after the flesh, not many mighty, not many noble are called.

Angel   Precisely. How true. Yes, gentlemen, you are indeed privileged. *(Leaves right. Caspar and Balthasar stare in bewilderment after him. Melchior goes on reading)*

Caspar   *(After a pause)* And what was all that about?

Melchior   I'm not sure. Another sign I think. *(Picks up a new magazine and reads. Caspar sits down in the middle of the row, exasperated and near the end of his tether)*

Balthasar   Not many wise. Mmm. Yes, it's true. And if the wise are called, it's not because of their wisdom. That can be a very fragile thing. I set out so conscious of my own learning and intellect: so sure of my interpretation of the truth. *(Pause)* It all just dropped away. In the end, I was just riding with my own inadequacies and doubts, and there was nothing left to do but keep riding.

Caspar   *(Stretching painfully)* Well, at least the riding is over for the present. The one good thing about this chair is that it is not a camel.

Balthasar *(Getting up with alacrity)* Ah, yes! I feel that if I never see another camel again it will be too soon! I think I would rather walk back!

Caspar Disagreeable they may be, uncomfortable they are, but we could not have done the journey without them. One has to admit the camel is a very reliable economic unit of transport.

Balthasar And the ugliest creature on earth! What possessed the Almighty to create a camel? The brute is the surliest animal known to man. It exerts itself only under threat, and with the worst possible grace, complaining loudly all the time. And if treated gently prefers to spit in your eye!

Melchior Perhaps we needed a reflection?

Balthasar *(Offended)* I? Surly and graceless?

Caspar You have done your share of complaining.

Balthasar I had cause! A man likes to be certain!

Caspar But then you were not suffering from galls and sleeping on the frozen ground. No, you had people to put up your tent, light your fires, unroll your bed in the most sheltered spot, leaving you with nothing to do but enjoy nursing your doubts.

Balthasar Are you suggesting my spiritual struggles made me blind to the physical suffering of others?

Caspar Yes! Especially mine. Talk of galls, *(rubs backside)* I have galls where galls have no right to be!

Balthasar turns away in a huff and stands with his back to them. A waiting pause

Melchior *(Reading from paper)* Dear me! I see the king is thinking of remarrying.

Caspar That's last year's.

Melchior Oh, is it? *(Peers at date)* So it is. I see they had a bad winter too. *(Another fidgety pause)*

Caspar *(To Balthasar)* Oh, forgive me. We have come too far together, and I'm not at my best when forced to sit idle and wait. I like to be doing something, bustling about, achieving things. And, to be honest, my organisation was not all I boasted, was it? The lack of shelters and the shortage of fuel. Hostile cities and unfriendly towns. It wasn't easy. *(To Melchior)* How you managed to stand up to all the hardships and the discomforts, I'll never know.

Balthasar softens and turns round

Melchior *(Still reading)* Mmmm?

Caspar But what has always puzzled me is why you came. You never really explained. When we were planning the whole thing, you simply rode up and said you wanted to come too. You've tagged along ever since. But why?

Melchior It seemed the only thing to do. *(Pause)* And I would do it again.

Balthasar Even though we are not sure why we have come? Even though it could all be a terrible waste of time?

Melchior Oh, it won't be that.

Balthasar How do you know? How can you be sure it won't be an appalling disappointment?

Melchior It depends on what you were expecting.

Balthasar Oh! Why, everything!

Melchior Then you will be disappointed. It is only the unexpected which is

never a disappointment. A shock maybe, but never a
disappointment.

*The Recording Angel bustles in from the right, still consulting his/her
clipboard*

Angel *(To him/herself)* Right. That's everyone then. Now we can . . .

*Caspar gets up and moves behind the Recording Angel, Balthasar
moves in front and he/she is hemmed in*

Caspar Yes. Right!

Balthsar We'd like to know what is happening and when we can go in!

Angel *(Surprised)* Of course, gentlemen. Very soon now. Won't keep you
long.

Caspar How long?

Balthasar We would like to be certain. Have we come to see a birth?

Angel Well, of course! This was the ordained birthplace.

Caspar Was? Then the child is born?

Balthasar Then when can we see him?

Angel In due time. In due time. I told you, gentlemen, there are others
before you with a prior claim.

Caspar *(Sardonically)* The "not very wise or mighty"?

Angel You could say that. Now, if you'll excuse me, gentlemen, I must go
and get ready. They'll be here at any moment. *(The Recording
Angel wriggles past them and exits hurriedly left. Melchior goes
back to his reading .Caspar and Balthasar face each other with*

looks of exasperation)

Caspar   Who do you suppose they are?

Balthasar   They could be that lot from Egypt. But they never travel. Think they know it all.

Caspar   Could they be Barbarians? They're not very noble.

Balthasar   No, no I think not. I have it! It will be those astrologers from Crete. Huh! It's like them to be late and then expect to take precedence. *(Sits down in the middle of the chairs)*

Caspar   *(Sitting down with a chair between them)* Oh, yes, I know the ones you mean. Small men with a fondness for messy divinations with entrails. Hmm, no, not very wise or noble. Still, I suppose we must be polite to them. Though why they should go first, heaven only knows!

Melchior   Sssh! I can hear singing. *(They listen)*

A far-off carol can be heard, sung in a rough and ready fashion to the accompaniment of a recorder or similar instrument. It becomes louder and louder and then breaks into shouts

This is it!

Are you sure?

We're here!

Yes, this is the one!

Get on with it then!

Let's get in out of the cold!

Alright! Stop shoving!

Come on then!

It should all be a jumble of cheery noise as the shepherds spill onto the stage from the right in an untidy flood. There must be at least four of them, preferably eight. They are all sizes and ages. Again, in the original production they were dressed traditionally, but they could equally be in modern caps, wellies, jackets and fleeces etc. They are exuberant and boisterous. Magazines and papers get scattered in the rush. They sit next to Balthasar and Caspar, squashing them and making their odours felt . . All in all, they overwhelm the wise men. One shepherd sits or crouches on the floor playing his recorder or, if in modern dress, a harmonica.

The following lines can be used in any order and certainly over-lapping and shouted

1 Here we are then!

2 . . . so I told him. Lock the gate. He never listens!

3 Hullo! Hullo! Who's this then?

4 Nice to be in out of the wind.

5 This is a turn up, 'n it?

6 Proper draughty tonight!

7 I reckon we woke up half the town.

8 All of it!

9 Don't they know? Haven't they heard?

10 Don't think we're the only ones. Couldn't be!

11   You never left Joe in charge? He'll be drunk in an hour!

12   We'll be back by then. This won't take long.

13   Who'd have thought?

14   You never know do you?

15   Oh, he'll be alright, if he doesn't fall asleep!

16   Amazin' 'n it?

17   That's right Charlie, give us a tune!

18   1 dunno when I've felt better!

19   You could've knocked me down with a feather!

20   'Ere we are then!

There is a sudden lull. Charlie stops playing

Balthasar   Good evening.

1st Shepherd   (*Sitting next to him*) Evening, Master!

Balthasar   Er, have you been waiting long?

1st Shepherd   Waiting? No! We didn't hang about. We came straight away.

Balthasar   Oh. (*Pause*) Did you have a good journey?

1st Shepherd   (*Puzzled*) Journey? Yes. I suppose so. Same as usual.

Caspar	How did you know? Did you have a sign?
1st Shepherd	Sign? *(Laughs uproariously)* Did you hear that? He wants to know if we had a sign?
2nd Shepherd	Did we have a sign? Did we have a sign? *(All the shepherds roar with laughter)*
Caspar	*(Puzzled and annoyed when the laughter dies down)* Well? Did you?
1st Shepherd	Yes.
Balthasar	How very interesting. And tell me, how did you interpret it?
1st Shepherd	Do what?
Balthasar	How did you explain it? How did you understand it?
2nd Shepherd	What was there to understand? We were just told and we came.
Balthasar	How wonderful! How I envy you. To be that certain.
1st Shepherd	Certain? Certain? Of course we're certain. *(Brief pause)* The only thing we weren't too sure about was the address.
Caspar	We had that problem too.
Balthasar	How long did your journey take you?
1st Shepherd	How . . . er . . . *(looks at others)* I dunno. How long would you reckon it took us?
2nd Shapherd	Oh, er . . . about ten minutes.

1st Shepherd Ten minutes.

2nd Shepherd No! Say . . . nearer twenty.

1st Shepherd Nearer twenty.

Balthasar *(Astonished)* Twenty minutes?

2nd Shepherd Could have been fifteen.

1st Shepherd Could have been fifteen.

Balthasar *(Bewildered)* Then . . . then you're not from Crete?

1st Shepherd Where's that?

Caspar You must be from round here then?

2nd Shepherd Bethlehem? Oh, yes. Born and bred not twenty minutes from here, or possibly fifteen.

Balthasar And . . . and how long have you known?

1st Shepherd Oh, er . . . *(to others)* how long do you reckon?

2nd Shepherd Half an hour.

1st Shepherd Half an hour.

Balthasar	*(Faintly)* Half an hour . . . ?
2nd Shepherd	Make that thirty five minutes.
1st Shepherd	Thirty five minutes.
Balthasar	You've only just found out. Here, right here! Half an . . . half an hour ago, and we, we've come from, dear God, it seems like the other side of the moon! All that way! All that planning and long, weary struggle and doubting . . .
Caspar	*(Looking at them closely)* You're not . . . not astrologers then?
1st Shepherd	Astrol . . . astr . . . ?
2nd Shepherd	Shouldn't think so, Master, whatever they are. We're shepherds.
Balthasar	*(Faintly)* Shepherds . . .
Melchior	*(Looking up from where he is putting the scattered papers and magazines back into a neat pile on the table)* Shepherds? Ah, the new dispensation, gentlemen. He hath put down the mighty from their seats and exalted them of low degree.
3rd Shepherd	Have you come to see the baby too?
Melchior	Yes. We've come to see the baby.
Caspar	And we were here first!
3rd Shepherd	Then it's true.

Melchior   What is?

3rd Shepherd   Good tidings for all people.

Melchior   If they will listen.

1st Shepherd   Listen? How could we help it? There was such an almighty crowd of them; my ears are still ringing!

Balthasar   *(Still shaken)* A sign . . . they were certain; and they came straightaway . . .

1st Shepherd   Well, we couldn't mess about, and it's got to be quick visit. We've only left Joe in charge.

2nd Shepherd   And he's as much use as a rabbit.

1st Shepherd   Yep, we can't leave them too long, not this time of year. Every man jack of us is needed.

Caspar   *(Humbled)* Every man jack of them is needed. You realise what this means, don't you? We could be spared. We could afford the long months of planning and the even longer nights of endless travelling. What do you suppose is going on in our absence? Are the people crying out for our return? I fool myself they can't manage without me, but when I return it will be as if I had never left. That's how much I am needed.

Melchior   No one needed me. That's why I was free to come.

The Recording Angel marches in briskly from the left

Angel   Ah, there you are! Right on time! Very satisfactory. *(All shepherds rise expectantly)*

1st   Are we going in now?
Shepherd

Angel   Right this minute!

               *The shepherds give a roaring cheer and begin to crowd off the
               stage left*

3rd   Alleluia! *(To Melchior)* Eh, Master?
Shepherd

Angel   Come along! Come along all of you! *(Caspar rises)* Er, no, not you
               gentlemen, not just yet. You will be next. Come along! *(Follows the
               shepherds out)*

               *Again the following lines can be used in an excited hubbub by the
               shepherds as they exit left*

1   Here we go then!

2   Can't believe this!

3   Amazin' 'n it?

4   Pity old Joe ain't here really.

5   Evenin' Masters!

6   Tell him when we get back.

7   They'll never believe this down the pub!

8   What a night! One to tell the grandchildren, eh?

9   Amazin' in it.

               Etc

The chattering stops abruptly as a door is closed. It is suddenly very quiet. Caspar stands looking after them indignantly. Balthasar sits

A pause

Melchior   *(Picks up a magazine to fan himself with)* Oooof! That warmed the place up a bit!

Caspar   Well!!! *(Sits down)*

Balthasar   *(Still looking left, longingly)* They are in there now. They are looking at him. They were certain.

Caspar   Well, we are certain too: certain to be in next. We'd better get ready. *(He reaches under his chair to bring out an object covered in a rich material)* What did you bring after all? I know you were undecided.

Balthasar   Incense. Frankincense to be precise.

Melchior   The aromatic gum resin of a tree.

Balthasar   Yes. The fruits of a tree: not to be eaten, but burnt. A sacrifice of praise. *(Awkwardly)* Well, it denotes worship. That's what I've come for after all. To worship.

Melchior   Sounds like a good choice.

Caspar   *(Getting out his gift)* Well, I'm a much more down to earth sort of person. I've brought the one thing that means the same in any culture - gold!

Melchior   And what does it mean?

Caspar   Oh! Er, well er . . . great wealth and er . . . power, I suppose.

Melchior Kingship.

Caspar Yes, yes. That's right, kingship. Yes, I like that. And what did you bring?

Melchior Myrrh.

Balthasar Myrrh?

Caspar That's a strange sort of gift, isn't it?

Melchior Another aromatic gum resin.

Caspar Yes, but isn't that associated with er, well, you know . . .

Melchior The dead? Yes.

Balthasar *(Sharply)* What exactly have we come to? A birth or a death?

Melchior I am old. I have seen many births and many more deaths. I had hoped . . . hoped . . . all out of darkness to find light.

Caspar And . . . ? *(A pause)*

Angel *(Entering briskly from left and smiling encouragingly)* Right, gentlemen!

Balthasar Is it our turn now?

Angel Nearly! Nearly! Just a few formalities first. *(Consults clipboard and prepares to write)*

Caspar *(Under his breath)* Bureaucrat!

Angel Now then, gentlemen. You saw the sign and you came straight here. Is that correct?

Balthasar   (*Looking at Caspar*) In a manner of speaking.

Caspar   (*Hurriedly*) After months of careful planning.

Angel   (*Writing*) Naturally. And apart from those you left behind in your own countries you have not spoken of your mission to anyone?

Caspar   Er . . .

Angel   (*Looking up sharply*) Well?

Caspar   Er . . .

Balthasar   There was that detour.

Angel   Ah, yes. Where exactly did you break your journey?

Melchior   (*Dryly*) Jerusalem.

Angel   Jerusalem?

Caspar   (*Rising*) It wasn't for long. It seemed only right you know, to pay my respects. After all, they are family. And then . . . and then, well, it seemed like a good place to ask. After all, we weren't sure.

Angel   (*Scandalised*) Not sure? You had the sign.

Balthasar   After that journey, our doubts were as large as our camels, and as ugly.

Angel   But to go round Jerusalem asking . . . What did you ask exactly?

Melchior   (*More dryly*) Where is he that is born King of the Jews?

Angel   (*Horrified*) You asked that in Jerusalem? (*Dreadful suspicion grips him/her*) Who exactly are your relatives in Jerusalem?

Balthasar The family of King Herod the Great.

Angel Herod? King Herod? Merciful heavens! You asked that of Herod the Great?

Caspar He was very helpful.

Angel Helpful?

Caspar Yes. He sent us here.

Angel Here! *(Staggers to a chair and sits)*

Balthasar *(Rising, concerned)* Yes. He summoned all his palace astrologers. It was very obliging of him really. They gave us the prophecy about Bethlehem. It was one we hadn't heard before.

Angel *(Moans)*

Melchior I don't think they believed us.

Angel What?

Melchior I don't think they took us seriously.

Caspar How can you say that?

Angel Yes. How can you say that?

Melchior It was what the King said, 'Go and search diligently for the child, and when, meaning if, you have found him, bring me word again that I too may come and worship him also'. You could tell, he was humouring us: three wise fools on a fool's errand.

Angel If only I could believe that. You don't know Herod, even if you are related to him. And that's a dangerous position to be in. A man who doesn't stop at murdering his own wife and son will not let three eccentric, wandering chieftains loose spreading rumour and speculation!

Balthasar   But if he doesn't believe it?

Angel   Belief? That has nothing to do with it. He hasn't got where he is today by leaving anything to chance. You will have been followed. Even now his messengers and spies will be on their way back to the palace to report on you and your journey's end.

Melchior   *(Rising)* Have we put the child's life in danger?

Angel   No. Not him. He was born to danger. *(His/her face is tragic for a moment)* No, it's the others I'm thinking about. *(The three wise men look at each other in bewilderment)* Right, this calls for a change of plan. *(Rising briskly)* Something of the sort was foreseen. But immediate action must be taken. Gentlemen, you must be ready the moment I send for you. *(Marches off left)*

Balthasar   You and your relations. All this way, for a fleeting glimpse.

Melchior   Well, we shall see for ourselves and end our doubts.

Caspar   I'm sorry. I will manage things. It seemed such a good idea at the time.

Melchior   A birth for some: more like a death for us. Certainly much of what we held dear has died within us. Pride of learning and intellect; pride of place and status. All these little personal gods we have been clutching, wrenched from us. The new dispensation, gentlemen, life through death.

Angel   *(Marching in briskly from left)* Right, gentlemen, if you are ready. They are waiting for you. As soon as possible, please. And I'm afraid you won't be able to stay long. They are already packing.

Balthasar   And after? That's strange. I never somehow envisaged an afterwards.

Angel Ah, yes. We can help you there with an alternative route. But it does mean going the long way round.

Caspar *(Groaning)* I never imagined there could be a longer way!

Angel Right then. As quickly as you can, please. *(Exits left)*

The three wise men look at each other with sudden tremendous expectation

Balthasar Gentlemen! The time has come at last.

Melchior The moment all my life has been leading up to.

Caspar The light over the horizon, leading into the dawn.

They form up into the traditional procession, facing left, holding their gifts high in front of them. Caspar first with the gold, Balthasar with the frankincense and Melchior with the myrrh

Caspar Are we ready, gentlemen?

Melchior Let us go forward.

They begin singing very slowly and solemnly, moving on the second line, very slowly

All We three kings of Orient are,
Bearing gifts we traverse afar,
Field and fountain,
Moor and mountain,
Following yonder st . . .

Recording Angel rushes in, furiously exasperated

Angel   Please, gentlemen! There isn't time for all that! (*Rushes out left*)

The three wise men look at each other and exit left as hurriedly as possible, singing very quickly

All   Oh, oh, star of wonder
Star of light!
Star with royal beauty bright,
Westward leading
Still procee . . .

A door slams shutting off the song

Slow curtain or blackout on an empty stage

End

Radius publications

Red Star by Les Ellison.
50 minutes, 5m, 6w/3m, 4w.
Yuri Gagarin, the first man in space, becomes a celebrity but loses control of his destiny.

Three Wise Fools by Margaret Franks.
35 minutes, 3m, 6 m/w.
The Wise Men encounter the Shepherds and reflect on the purpose of their journey.

Cell Talk by Dana Bagshaw.
1 hour, 2w.
The mystics Julian of Norwich and Margery Kempe talk about life, love and God.

Iscariot by Michael Hendy.
1 hour, 4m, 2w.
Judas is tried in a modern court for his part in the Crucifixion.

Divine Judgement: a study course by Derek Davidson.
Five study sessions introduce discussion topics suggested by Michael Hendy's Iscariot.

These publications are available at £5+£1 p&p. Please note that the postage cost should be repeated for each item.

Please send completed form to:
Radius
NODA House
58-60 Lincoln Road
Peterborough PE1 2RZ
t 01733 565 613
e info@radius.org.uk

Order form

	No of copies	Cost @ £5	P&P @ £1	Total
Red Star				
Three Wise Fools				
Cell Talk				
Iscariot				
Divine Judgement				
Total	*I enclose a cheque payable to Radius for*			

Name _____ Mr/Mrs/Ms/Rev

Address _____

Postcode _____